ALSO BY LINDA GREGG

Too Bright to See
(poems)

ALMA

ALMA

LINDA GREGG

RANDOM HOUSE   NEW YORK

Portions of this work were first published
in the following publications:
*The American Poetry Review, Crazyhorse,
Columbia: A Magazine of Poetry and Prose, The Iowa Review,
The Kenyon Review, The New Yorker, The Paris Review,
Parnassus: Poetry in Review, Pequod, Ploughshares, Sonora Review,*
and *The Virginia Quarterly Review.*

The following poems first appeared in *Ironwood*:
"Alma Thinking about Men" (as "Coming Back"), "The Copperhead,"
"How the Joy of It Was Used Up Long Ago," "The River Again and Again,"
"Marriage and Midsummer's Night," "What They Ate What They Wore,"
"Winter Birds," "The Thing Being Made," and "Pressure against Emptiness."

"Coming Home" and "Lovers" first appeared in
Tendril magazine (Fall 1985, #21).

Library of Congress Cataloging in Publication Data

Gregg, Linda.
Alma.

I. Title.
PS3557.R433A79   1985   811'.54   85-2224
ISBN 0-394-54688-1
ISBN 0-394-74127-7 (pbk.)

Manufactured in the United States of America

Designed by JoAnne Metsch

BVG 01

The author wishes to thank the
John Simon Guggenheim Foundation for
their generous fellowship, which allowed
her the time to finish this book.

For my mother,
Frances Rundall Gregg

CONTENTS

ALMA

THE SCENT OF WHITE

The old ox and the ancient woman labor mightily
up the mountain with the strength of perishing.
The strength of each time maybe the last.
She hums and they blur into energy.
The mountain busies in the heat for their coming,
making an offering of herself. Up they walk,
up into the tall gown of the mountain that shows
her nakedness passionate. Dry scent of thyme
and sage and the smell of passing away.
The faint colors of white. Occasionally color
like fierce hunger, pomegranate or broom-yellow.
Emptiness as she waits, occasioned all summer
by nothing but goats.

AT HOME

Far is where I am near.
Far is where I live.
My house is in the far.
The night is still.
A dog barks from a farm.
A tiny dog not far below.
The bark is soft and small.
A lamp keeps the stars away.
If I go out there they are.

ME AND APHRODITE
AND THE OTHER

She doesn't move and she is stronger than I am.
She makes sounds like winter. When I plead
that I can't hear, she doesn't hear
because of the power coming out of her.
She isn't pretty. Her strength is by will.
Her mind is kept small.

Maybe those months on the mountain were too much.
Aphrodite loved me and I loved her back.
Taking her pomegranates each time I climbed
that starkness. I would search all day
in the heat and would sit finally happy
in the shade of the fig tree with what
I had found of her scant, broken treasures,
the goat bells clattering around as I looked
down through her light to the Aegean. In a daze
of weariness, reverence and clarity.

Now this older one has come. More ancient,
tougher, less complete and as fine as can be.
She has come thinking I am strong enough,
though I sit on the curbs crying
without knowledge, without control.
Sees my mouth open and my agony.
If she can, she will destroy my life.
If she can't, I'll try again to be married.

ME AND ALMA

Time holds us together with a strong hand.
Nothing is allowed to go away on its own.
Not fish, snow nor grass.
All must issue one from the other.
This woman is my flesh, my heavy bones.
She turns as if I am the tree
and Alma its leaves.
I the green the wind of her is undoing.
Soon there will be nothing so different together
as she and I. Stone and water, dirt and fern.

ALMA THINKING ABOUT MEN

I stood watching the great hulk of desire
glide within memory. Watched it move
like the only true beauty in the world. Let it pass.
Kept to the ragged path the old men made
one by one and long ago. Desire would have led me away.
My heart beats within the galaxy of this life—
restrained, limited, in love.
Understanding how some siren longings kill.
I, keeping still in my distance, surprise them
by holding my ground, singing and shouting down praise
upon them. As if I were one of them.
I, the girl who ate dirt, who wrote of the fool
hidden in the straw crying because he wanted a monkey
and some bells to make a living.
I, who looked at the drying leaves with my heart,
have learned to come back.

DAYS

Moon is hobbled and placed in a field.
Listens to cicadas and watches the cripple
walk to the restaurants to play his bagpipe
for what little they give. The goats with her
bleat and jump happily on the rocks.
She looks at the mountains she knew
and feels like weeping, but does not.
Eats leaves from the fig tree that grows
over the wall. Her reaching up and pulling
rings the bell around her neck. Maybe,
she thinks, it's the beginning of something.

SAFE AND BEAUTIFUL

Moon, you are getting worse and worse.
Lying around in pretty satin,
your hair fixed all careful like a widow.
I capture this lizard and house it
in my hands. Feel the scratching.
We look at each other between my fingers,
he as Dante and I as the ghost,
the Lost-in-the-Night, the daughter
of faith built on common ground. While you,
old moon, play safe, safe, beautiful and safe.

THE GHOSTS POEM

I

Heavy black birds flying away hard from trees
which are the color of rust that will green.
A smaller bird says his life is easy.
"I can fly over the water and return.
I feel very little. I see to it the dead
in the boats keep their arms crossed
in the correct position. They are shaken
by wind and the drift to leeward.
And when they arrive, I am there by the lilies.
I sing my highest song. They open their eyes
and memory is removed from them.
It is the final condition."

II

I used to skate on the pond and now it is water.
With the sound of hammers and scythes, scythes
and hammers all around. So what do I know?
Laurie is dying. She told her husband she's tired
of fighting. He said he'll be glad when it's over.
They are giving her a mixture of heroin and morphine
so the mother says goodbye to her friends in euphoria.
What does she see? The Acropolis in moonlight before
it decreases? The kore which resembles most of what
we have to offer? Does death carry us to speak
with the invisible? Are we carried to an ocean
where water covers our feet and then withdraws,
leaving us shivering? What does history have to say?
"Empty rooms. The dead in layers."

III

Ghosts and the old are gathered here.
Bored of being gathered without waltzes,
one asks for music and the bird says soon.
Spider comes and goes in her tunnel.
Lady, I ask, is it true you are cruel?
You are very busy. Do you make coverings
for us to wear? "I work for Death
and the power of men. If you want me less,
you know what to do," she answers.
But I am not persuaded. The sight of them
blind and groping fills me with pain.
I must help them down the stairs and on
their way. They are the best we had,
and among them are the bronze bells
of that deliberate passion which saves
what is perfection from ruin.

IV

I go to the shore and say to Death,
here I am. What power do you have
if I care only for the living?
He shows me his skirt to be inviting.
He sings his loudest song. I sing low.
Death, I sing, you are not dear.
You are nothing but a hole in the ground.
"Watch your mouth," says the spider.
But I am too excited and tell him I have
music and memories. That men and women
embrace even in stone on the old tombs.

V

Dirt road. Then under tall pines. Then grass.
Where the land slopes, the sun shines
and many flowers came up. Some right away,
some later, some finally.
Wild in that place which had been a pond.
There is a creek, and a dark hill of trees
beyond, with ferns from spring until October.
Last year I spent time there every day.
I weeded out the briars and my hands bled.
During the summer there were many snakes,
or one often. This is not a story.
This is how I lived. Morning glories covered
the wall, poppies lasted late into autumn.
This winter, when the snow thawed a little,
I saw through the ice the pansies.
They still had green leaves and stems
and the flowers were the same color as before.

VI

The blackness at the window turned me back
to the fire. My heart praised its warmth
and the sound it makes of a snake hissing,
as a man breathes out when struck. The room was
darkest in the corners where the ghosts were.
What is alive is everything, they said.
Death has you standing still, little sister.
We can help very little. Bird is the least
useful. Spider is really an old woman
who hides in the ground because she is poor.
But snake knows death. He has it both ways.
Escapes from his body and lives again.
His divisions and endings return on themselves.
See how he comes into the bright summer garden
when he has a choice. Snake is wonderful.

VII

There must be more than just emotion.
Longing is enough to get me where I am,
but it cannot change me from a plant
that sings into a snake which sleeps
like a doe in the sun and then slides
into the blackness we balk from.
The resonance of romance brightens
the invisible so it can be seen.
We must ascend into light to be manifest.

VIII

If we did not hold so much, I would not write.
If it were not for memories, for the ghosts
carrying the hundred clamoring moons,
I would be safe. The forests keep
saying I should not remember, but always
there is the sound of their breathing.
If it were all right just to love and die,
I would not be in this empty place
three stories up looking out on nothing
I know. If I could bind my mouth
or teach my heart despair of living,
I would not be here learning what to say.

THE NIGHT BEFORE LEAVING

We sit at the kitchen table
waiting for some opening.
For the proper handling
of goodbye.
Going deeper and deeper
into the hours, like slow divers
sinking in their heavy gear.
We look at each other, gesturing
which way to go
through the lamplight,
garbage bags, dishes in the sink
and on the table.
We surface in a kind of dream.
The boat touches ground.
Grinds onto the rocks.
We get out,
and it floats again.

MARRIAGE AND MIDSUMMER'S NIGHT

It has been a long time now
since I stood in our dark room looking
across the court at my husband in her apartment.
Watched them make love.
She was perhaps more beautiful
from where I stood than to him.
I can say it now: She was like a vase
lit the way milky glass is lighted.
He looked more beautiful there
than I remember him the times
he entered my bed with the light behind.
It has been ten years since I sat
at the open window, my legs over the edge
and the knife close like a discarded idea.
Looked up at the Danish night,
that pale, pale sky where the birds that fly
at dawn flew on those days all night long,
black with the light behind. They were caught
by their instincts, unable to end their flight.

WINTER BIRDS

Tell me a riddle, I said, that has no answer.
That will hold us to each other fast
and forever, like dumb things
which cannot grow, that do not change us.
That let us stay here together.
What makes a web of the winter? you said.
What are the trees of the dead?
What wind blows through all that
as the moon begins her ending, her ending?
you sang. And we danced in the cow-vacant night.
Dancing and singing until our hearts grew fat.

BALANCING EVERYTHING

When I lie in bed thinking of those years, I often
remember the ships. On the Aegean especially.
Especially at night among the islands or going
to Athens. The beauty of the moon and stillness.
How hard those journeys sometimes were.
The powerful smell of vomit and urine, sweetened
coffee and crude oil when the ship struggled
against the wind. I think of the night
we were going to die in the storm trying to reach
the passenger liner. Huge waves smashing
over our little boat. Jack screaming at the captain
because he hit me in his fear. Old Greek women
hiding their heads in my lap. Like a miracle.
I talked to them with the few words I knew.
Simple things. How it would be all right.
Telling them to look at the lights of their village
at the top of the great cliffs of Santorini,
up in the dark among the stars.

THE VISITOR

She comes in and sees winter and him
alone in the apartment.
Sits at the table thinking of when
they had lived together. Seeing
what her life was like now.
Thinks how often gentleness means suffering.
She looks out at the panel of snow.
A bird lands on a wire.
He says it is a starling.
"Fat, dark bird," she says and feels sad.
It goes away and comes back.
And goes away completely.
The man has come to see her
bringing his life. To a place
she does not yet belong.
Now her life is divided between him
and John. She looks at the snow
and thinks of her warmth and its meaning.
She puts the curtain down over the dark
before returning to the man in Amherst.

FIGURES NEAR A BRIDGE

Everything formal.
The man turns around
and makes a sound.
It is a long cry.
The woman turns around
so you can see her face.
The look on her face
is the sound he made.

PICTURES OF MARRIAGE

I

It is the way Arnolfini holds his wife's hand
that helps me. His under hers.
It's not the fancy bed nor them facing us.
I am in love with their simply being together,
even so formally. Human even so.
The dance-like way they hold still. As if she
had just lifted the skirt so their feet might
begin to step in the nice music of that time.

II

The potato-eaters move according to an absence
of music. They sit so close around the table,
it's as if the hands could be exchanged.
The man's for the woman's, the boy's for the mother's.
Any of them for the tree outside.
The gnarled one with limbs cut back so often
it seems to have wanted to hold more than it can.
The same way, somehow, that Van Gogh does not turn
from what is turned from. Not even
from those in the dim light who fold into each other,
into what they dig up to eat. Into that music.

FORGET ALL THAT

I don't want to confuse the world
any more with songs about love.
They sound like the giant creakings
of a wooden ship that never comes
into port these days. And even if
there was one, we would be lost
before they decided who should board.
No, the air is vast on bright days,
and the sea full of myths and miseries
loose there in the transparent dark
like some relaxed dead thing pulled
and pushed. No, let us stop telling
each other stories about love.
Of naked bodies facing each other in
the room lit only because another is.
(How quietly and slowly they approach!)
Let us leave out those visions. My job
is to keep finding quiet rooms in this city.
To know one move ahead so when the owner
arrives I have a sense of real direction
as I walk to the next one,
and the one after.

NOR THE MOON NOR PRETEND

If this woman is simple
do you love her less?
Is she less important?
If she looks like sadness
but is love itself
do you want not to see her?
If you see only face and hair,
don't you imagine the hands
lifted in some larger scene?
Can't you tell she will last
until the world is done?

ALMA IN THE WOODS

I show them how the snow melts from the stone
before it goes from the ground. Show them my joy
without reason over this. I show them my passion
for the white birches on the upper ground.
That whiteness in the midst of gray maples.
Those tender trees among the winter-wise evergreens.
I tell them of being seventeen and alone,
on my hands and knees with my mouth to the stream
like a deer. Not strange, but unseen.
Waking to the woods always, and that sound.
I tell them how it can be wild high in the trees
and quiet underneath where I go to see things
which are dead and singing. Seeking with my mouth
what is lowest and most forlorn. I go where moss
and ferns give themselves to my ignorance,
making a song of themselves for me. And I sing back,
making songs from the bones of belief.

THE THING BEING MADE

Everything is black. From a distance
a figure is coming. It could be a man
but it is a woman. She is walking
wearing a kimono. She is so white
it is as if she were left unpainted.
An absence all over her. Whole but unfinished.
She turns to her left and lifts both arms,
touching her hands to her mouth.
I can't tell if she is grieving.
On the right is the sea in the blackness.
(I can tell by the noise of its hurrying.)
There is a moon, but it does not shine.
The color of old aluminum. I have seen
bright dolphins arched for a moment each,
their bodies above their dark world.

AT THE GATE IN THE MIDDLE OF MY LIFE

I had come prepared to answer questions,
because it said there would be questions.
I could have danced or sung. Could have loved.
But it wanted intelligence. Now it asks
what can be understood but not explained
and I have nothing with me. I take off
my shoes and say this is a plate of food.
I say the wind is going the wrong way.
Say here is my face emerging into clear light
that misses the sea we departed from to join you.
Take off my jacket and say this is a goat alone.
It embraces me, weeping human tears. Dances
sadly three times around. Then three times more.

SAYING GOODBYE TO THE DEAD

I walk on the dirt roads being my father.
Between tobacco fields empty in February
except for the wooden stakes and the wires.
The earth is spongy after the rains
which washed the snow away. Dogs bark
near the houses around the fields.
Mountains beyond that. I clap my hands
in the air over my head, four times.
Turn on one foot around with my arms lifted.
Stop and look at the sky fast and hard.
Then walk to the bakery and buy day-old
sweet rolls to eat in my room at the hotel.

NOT SAYING MUCH

My father is dead and there is nothing left
now except ashes and a few photographs.
The men are together in the old pictures.
Two generations of them working and boxing
and playing fiddles. They were interested
mostly in how men were men. Muscle and size.
Played their music for women and the women
did not. The music of women was long ago.
Being together made the men believe somehow.
Something the United States of America could
not give them. Not even the Mississippi.
Not running away or the Civil War or farming
the plains. Not exploring or the dream of gold.
The music and standing that way together
seems to have worked. They married women
the way they made a living. And the women
married them back, without saying much,
not loving much, not singing ever.
Those I knew in California lived and died
in beauty and not enough money. But the beauty
was like a face with the teeth touching
under closed lips and the eyes still. The men
did not talk to them much, and neither time
nor that fine place gave them a sweetness.

OEDIPUS EXCEEDING

Finally Oedipus came back. Returned
as the old to the ancient. Found a stone
and sat down. Blind and blinding.
Slowly people gathered around him,
hesitant and horrified. He began.

The earth is winnowed, he said.
Put through a sieve. It is what happens
at the borders. A grinding away.
The ocean against the curving shore.
Sky against the mountain. Less rock.
Fewer trees. A reduction of whatever
bulges. A hammering.

Almost nothing of it is useful to us.
The ocean and sky laboring to make
their place. Salt wetness and the storm.
If we go forward, we go beyond.
If we return to the gentle green center,
we come back defeated. We are expected
to rejoice and grieve at the same moment.

A telling goes on at the border.
At the border an intermingling of fish
with swallow. Of eagle with hands.
I have returned to mix my blood with our
earth. Mix myself with what we are not.
(His voice in the crowd was like wind

blowing the chaff away.) There is a hole
in the ground behind this stone, he said,
through the bushes. I will go there now
and lie down forever.

The people walked back toward town.
Something had happened. Everything
was sacred. Air, goat, plants, people.
All full of worship. Bodies, torsos, legs,
minds full of worship. And strong enough
to be happy in the elements.

THE SHOPPING-BAG LADY

You told people I would know easily what the murdered
lady had in her sack which could prove she was happy
more or less. As if they were a game, the old women
who carry all they own in bags, maybe proudly,
without homes we think except the streets.
But if I could guess (nothing in sets for example),
I would not. They are like those men who lay their
few things on the ground in a park at the end of Hester.
For sale perhaps, but who can tell? Like her way
of getting money. Never asking. Sideways and disconcerting.
With no thanks, only judgment. "You are a nice girl,"
one said as she moved away and then stopped in front
of a bum sitting on the bench who yelled that he would
kill her if she did not get away from him. She walked
at an angle not exactly away but until she was the same
distance from each of us. Stood still, looking down.
Standing in our attention as if it were a palpable thing.
Like the city itself or the cold winter. Holding her hands.
And if there was disgrace, it was God's. The failure
was ours as she remained quiet near the concrete wall
with cars coming and the sound of the subway filling
and fading in the most important place we have yet devised.

LIES AND LONGING

Half the women are asleep on the floor
on pieces of cardboard.
One is face down under a blanket
with her feet and ankle bracelet showing.
Her spear leans against the wall by her head
where she can reach it.
The woman who sits on a chair won't speak
because this is not her dress.
An old woman sings an Italian song in English
and says she wants her name in lights:
Faye Runaway. Tells about her grown children.
One asks for any kind of medicine.
One says she has a rock that means honor
and a piece of fur.
One woman's feet are wrapped in rags.
One keeps talking about how fat she is
so nobody will know she's pregnant.
They lie about getting letters.
One lies about a beautiful dead man.
One lies about Denver. Outside
it's Thirtieth Street and hot and no sun.

HOW THE JOY OF IT
WAS USED UP LONG AGO

No one standing.
No one for a long time.
The room is his room,
but he does not go there.
Because of the people.
He stands in the dark hall.
The smell makes him close
his eyes, but not move
from the place so near.
They have cut the cow open
and climb into the ooze·
and pulse of its great body.
The man is noble, the festival
growing louder in his flesh.
His face is sad with thinking
of how to think about it,
while his mind is slipping
into the fat woman.
The one he saw for a moment
near day, open and asleep.
A filth on the floor of that room.

WHAT THEY ATE WHAT
THEY WORE

We see the dog running
and it excites us dimly
as if our lives were important.
The living dog and not
the idea of having one.
Like when my mind sees them
building that great wall
through China and I wonder
where they slept. Huts
with reed roofs or caves in stone.
And what they thought it meant.
I was telling an old farmer
who gave me a ride last month
I might have a job picking apples.
Be sure to wear gloves, he said.
The apples are very cold in the morning.

COMING HOME

I see no way to survive the soul's journey.
At the beginning, we are like angels
painted around the Madonna. Conceived
in safety, in the freshness of our bodies.
As we age, wisdom can be heard climbing
the stairs blindly under the bare bulb
groping for a string which we know how
to find in the dark only if we have
practiced delicately meanwhile.

THE MEN LIKE SALMON

The heart does not want to go up.
The bones whip it there, driving it
with a terrible music of the spirit.
The flesh falls off like language,
bruised and sick. Sick with the bones.
Rotten with sorrow. Leaving everything
good or loved behind. The bones
want to go. To end like Christ.
Ah, the poor flesh. The mute sound
of flesh against stone. Emptied
of maidens and summer and all
the fine wantonness of life.
The bones insist on immaculate changes.
The women stand to the side remembering
Io with vicious flies close to her heart.

LOVERS

He keeps her away, thinking they know each other
too much. Thinking it will be good again with her
if he stays away long enough again.
As in the old days when they knew nothing
of each other and were intimate,
as one enters a field of wind alone.
She makes songs and things and is pleased
but understands that angels sad and poor fill
the place of absence, of people, and of lovers
if there were any. Lovers, as the wind calls
desire and means those who never know each other.

THE COPPERHEAD

Almost blind he takes the soft dying
into the muscle-hole of his haunting.
The huge jaws eyeing, the raised head sliding
back and forth, judging the exact place of his killing.
He does not know his burden. He is not so smart.
He does not know his feelings. He only knows
his sliding and the changing of his hunger.
He waits. He sleeps. He looks but does not know his
seeing. He only knows the smallness of a moving.
He does not see the fear of the trapping.
He only sees the moving. He does not feel the caution.
He does not question. He only feels the flexing
and rearing of his wanting. He goes forward
where he is eyeing and knows the fastness
of his mouthing. He does not see the quickness collapsing.
He does not see at all what he has done. He only feels
the newness of his insides. The soft thing moving.
He does not see the moving. He is busy coaxing
and dreaming and feeling the softness moving in him.
The inside of him feels like another world.
He takes the soft thing and coaxes it
away from his small knowing. He would turn in and follow,

hunt it deep within the dark hall of his fading knowing,
but he cannot. He knows that.

That he cannot go deep within his body for the finding
of the knowing. So he slows and lets go. And finds
with his eyes a moving. A small moving that he knows.

DEATH LOOKS DOWN

Death looks down on the salmon.
A male and a female in two pools, one above
the other. The female turns back along the path
of water to the male, does not touch him,
and returns to the place she had been.

I know what death will do. Their bodies already
are sour and ragged. Blood has risen
to the surface under the scales. One side
of his jaw is unhinged. Death will pick them up.
Put them under his coat against his skin
and belt them there. Will walk away
up the path through the bay trees.
Through the dry grass of California to where
the mountain begins. Where a few deer
almost the color of the hills will look up
until he is under the trees again and the road ends
and there is a gate. He will climb over that
with his treasure. It
will be dark by then.

But for now he does nothing. He does not disturb
the silence at all. Nor the occasional sound
of leaves, of ferns touching, of grass or stream.
For now he looks down at the salmon large and whole
motionless days and nights in the cold water.
Lying still, always facing the constant motion.

Apollo's left fist covers his heart.
His eyes are holes. He used to shine,
but time has darkened him.
His bronze thighs are covered with words.
He is waist-deep in language.
I see wheat, lust-teacher, tree-darkness.
Goat, mountain, river, tree-in-a-field.
Was he merged with life?
Was he ripeness holding still?
Did he say, this is my body, eat me?
Was he strength made out of pity?
He has the pierced, blank look of love,
knowing we die as flowers do
and it makes a difference, a pressure
against emptiness. Did they know him?
Did the shining change their bones?
At night they knew the grass by touch.
When day began to end they heard owls.
Away in the fields and within their bodies.

CHOOSING AGAINST RUINS

I thought the old statue was a kore,
but it's probably Artemis.
Either of them is almost gone.
Love has worn her down to mere stone,
past her time of clarity.
Rough to the breasts and then smooth
down to the feet.
She has stopped being a woman,
is a generality of form.
Which does not delight me nowadays.
I have returned to the ocean
too many times to care what survives
the rising or fails the thrust.
It was flourishing she stayed for:
made briefly moon-bright under
the sycamore tree by the brook
to give strength to the world.
That time came and passed.
She grew into a woman.
Stood quiet and straight.
Then rain fell. The rain fell and fell.
Now there is only a possibility
she remains. A shadow of stone.

INNOCENTS

The dahlias are tied up straight
in the German garden in Russia
and the mistress is walking there
with small steps. Ah, someone is
always managing. Not the very rich,
but one of the servants.
Poor Akim has lost everything
and now is called drunk because
of his grief by the pious man
who has given him a lift in the cart.
After two days the cart comes on
Akim's wife who throws herself crying
on the ground saying he should kill her.
Saying the man she ran off with
took her and then threw her away.
That was the man who ruined Akim.
She thought it was love. Yesterday
the moon came up red, making a dark shade
for the lovers. The man came out of it
rich all in one day. Maybe the moon
is like the servant in a stiff white hat
who manages the rich lady. Who in turn
manages the son who orders cruelty
for those who have suffered the most
and have nothing.

WHAT IS LEFT OVER

There is silence after a city is destroyed
the Russian woman told me. For those left,
there are potatoes which might grow soon
enough. No pigeons and no rats. All eaten.
The brother who died was eating cooked water
from a spoon that distant morning.
Josef, hearing it again, cut his hand
and the party ended. The vodka was drunk
and the two kinds of caviar eaten.
I never understood what they were celebrating
in the first place. He told me to go up
and get into his bed. He was talking Russian
angrily at her as I went up the stairs.
She had said the city was like a stage set
for the few people. That her mother built
a shed against the palace portico,
keeping her eyes on the garden so no one
could steal the potato plants.

SOMETHING SCARY

Over the phone Joel tells me
his marriage is suddenly miraculous.
That his wife is glad now about us.
Is even grateful.
"We have crossed a border," he says.
I listen, knowing myself too far gone
to last more than a day.
Remembering him in that dark room
with the shades down saying,
"You don't need the sun. You carry
a brightness in you." And me saying
nothing, burning alone lying there
like the terrible brightness of heaven.

NEW YORK ADDRESS

The sun had just gone out
and I was walking three miles to get home.
I wanted to die.
I couldn't think of words and I had no future
and I was coming down hard on everything.
My walk was terrible.
I didn't seem to have a heart at all
and my whole past seemed filled up.
So I started answering all the questions
regardless of consequence:
Yes I hate dark. No I love light. Yes I won't speak.
No I will write. Yes I will breed. No I won't love.
Yes I will bless. No I won't close. Yes I won't give.
Love is on the other side of the lake.
It is painful because the dark makes you hear
the water more. I accept all that.
And that we are not allowed romance but only its distance.
Having finished with it all, now I am not listening.
I wait for the silence to resume.

I WILL REMEMBER

I will remember making love last night.
I thought when you rolled on your back
we would not. You halted my hand
on your arm, just touching my fingers.
But then something happened and we were
all of a sudden part of the same weight.

ALMA IN THE DARK

She reaches over and puts a hand on his hipbone
and presses. He turns softly away and she makes
his shape against the back. Her arm around
the waist covering his unguarded stomach.
He does not wake. Her heart in its nest
sings foolishly. It is awake and happy
and useless at this time. Saying dumb things
like *The stone house is firm*
or *The almond tree is blown around in the wind.*

The lamb was so skinny I thought it was a baby goat
and called my sister to see. Lying on his side,
legs straight out in front, little stomach pulsing.
The head lifted, sideways, and began telling us
how much he hated the promiscuous sun which shines
on all things equally. Rotting one, growing strength
in another. On those caged in virtue and on men who
walk through the streets at ease in the hot light.
On that which is not quite animal, on what is not
quite mineral. That which hisses in the shadows
along the wall. Army of horses practicing formations
in the Swiss mountains. Shepherds fleeing into Italy.
On two dead fish on the sidewalk still pink from
their life in the sea. Finally the lamb slept.
The trees on the hills around us were silent.
Inside everything was moving, shivering with wind.

DRY GRASS & OLD COLOR OF THE FENCE & SMOOTH HILLS

The women are at home in this California town.
The eucalyptus trees move against whiteness.
When a mother comes by I touch the child's face
over and over, sliding my hand lightly down,
and each time he smiles. All life is beautiful
at a distance. But when I sit in their houses,
it's all mess and canning and babies crying.
I hear over and over the stories about their men:
betrayal, indifference, power. Age without passion,
boys without fathers. My sister lives between.
She cleans her house. She names all the roses
she shows me. She turns on the record and we dance.
She inside with the door open, me on the porch.
Later her boyfriend arrives. The one who hits her,
and steals her money, and gets drunk. Etcetera.
They have sex. In the morning we're alone and she
wants to know if I want waffles with raspberry jam.

There's nothing gentle where Aphrodite was.
Empty mountain and grasshoppers banging
into me. Maybe there never was.
But I go up again and again to search
under thornbushes and rocks.
Am grateful for the marble arm
big as my thumb. A shard with a man's feet
and a shard with the feet of a bird. A sign
that it can be more. Like when a wind comes
in the great heat and lifts at my body.
Like when I get back to my mountain, aching
and my hands hurt. Sit alone looking down at
evening on the ocean, drinking wine or not.

IF DEATH WANTS ME

If death wants me, let it come.
I am here in a room at night on my own.
The pulsing and the crickets would go on.
Everything and the tall trees bathed in darkness
would continue. I am here with the lights on
writing my last words. If he does not come,
I will still be here doing the same thing.
Things change outside of me. Rain is falling
fast in the quiet. My love got on a boat
and it went away. I stayed. When the moon rose,
I tilted my head to the side when she did.
When people came, I felt a little crazy.
I did what I remembered. Made food.
Asked questions and responded. And they left.
I would go to sleep and wake in the sun.
Love the day as if it were a host of memories,
then go to the wall and wait.
That hour was perhaps the finest of all.
No people. No bright face. No geese walking home.
No night sounds at all. I was silent
with all things around coming and leaving
in abeyance on their journeying. I would sing
a song for them all. This is for you
and this is for you. And then the moon would slide up
over the hill and I would be captured in her light
like a growing thing, gone and complete.

THE RIVER AGAIN AND AGAIN

If we stayed together long enough to see
the seasons return, to see the young animals
and the opening of peonies and summer heat,
then we could make sense of the hawk's calm
or the deer. I could show you how repetition
helps us to understand the truth.
And we would know one another sometimes
with a love that touches indifference.

WITH A BLESSING RATHER
THAN LOVE SAID NIETZSCHE

The square stone room makes a shape in the air
to rest inside. A form for holding what is loved
beyond naming. With gratitude and reverence
as Nietzsche. We have other ways,
other places. Like figs left on the stone shelf
above the patio as a gift.
You go out and return with fruit you've picked
and I make jam for our crepes and yogurt
and we eat. It is still morning and we look
at each other even though we have known each other
for years. You take me on your lap
in the chair by the open window and pull off
the shirts over our heads so we can feel the air
and embrace and kiss high up on the mountain
in the shaded room by the screen window
where the air comes in and keeps touching us
and we are happy beyond saying, beyond
any sounds even. Less than nothing and deeper.

LESSENING

Without even looking in the album
I realized suddenly, two months later,
you had stolen the picture of me.
The one in color in the Greek waves.
After you had hurt me so much,
how could you also take the picture
from me of a time before I knew you?
When I was with Jack.
Steal the small proof that once
I lived well, was loved
and beautiful.

WHITE LIGHT

Waiting in a place where the cicadas turn the silence
into something silver. Hot light on the rocks.
Laurel down by the spring. Holding myself still.
Doing one thing at a time. Drink water, burn paper,
wash floor. The sun makes me lower my eyes to see
when I am outdoors. Wind turns the leaves
hour after hour. View of water far below.
Town far below by the water.
Sky beyond the next island.
Loneliness goes out as far as I can see.

ADULT

I've come back to the country where I was happy
changed. Passion puts no terrible strain on me now.
I wonder what will take the place of desire.
I could be the ghost of my own life returning
to the places I lived best. Walking here and there,
nodding when I see something I cared for deeply.
Now I'm in my house listening to the owls calling
and wondering if slowly I will take on flesh again.

STILL, ATTENTIVE, CLENCHED

The fir, poplar and eucalyptus around the house
move each in its own way in the same wind.
Then a man comes easily through the trees
with some urgent duty, like Hermes with his orders
memorized. He is fearsome because he does not care
about me personally. Merely wants.
He calls and I do not answer. It is like war.
He knocks on the door and I slide down the wall.
Hug my knees, hear my breathing. He walks around
to the windows and I lie on my stomach.
He calls my name. He does not tell me why he has come.
The lights are out, but he can see the fire is burning.
I know he knows I am there. Knows how much I am afraid.

NOT WANTING HERSELF

Not wanting herself, she tries to go
into whatever makes longing:
the hawks mating and falling,
the Sung paintings where the Chinese
live in their own distance.
Wrenching to get away,
she puts down money
to go into the dark place
and see advertisements of her desires.
But they hit her. Hit her
when she wanted to see the birds fly.
Birds who are part of herself
with hearts you can eat.
They invade her longing
with an intelligence that does not hold
on to anything. Ah, dreams,
she is losing even you.
The only lover her mind has left
separates her mind like milk.

SASKIA AND ALMA GO
DIFFERENT WAYS

My life was already desperate when she got sick.
When Saskia lay down that night, she was wet
under the chin and she might die. She was weak
and her teeth showed. She didn't push against me
with her feet. She didn't eat my hair.

My feet were bare when I saw her dead.
My blanket was still warm when I took her down
the wooden steps to the grass and the fig tree
and buried her in the ground. I was on my hands
and knees putting what I love over the body.
A leaf fell on her from the tree.

I hold on to so many things. When I lived on the island,
I climbed the vacant mountain again and again
to put fruit on the rocks where Aphrodite had been.
My friend Michiko sat gentle at her table
under the cypress on the other mountain and did not live
long after she left. I hold my mother, the earth and cows.
We go by ship, bicycle, by owl to get beyond ourselves,
beyond this world. To include the other, and fail.

Or get only a little. I carry ashes across this snow
and dump them on the place that will sink down
when the whiteness is gone. Some of the ashes blow
a small distance, making a stain. I remember
the woman in Kurosawa's film after they lost the battle
with something on her back looking for people

she knew by their absence, as the planet was found
because of the force of the invisible.

I sat in Portsmouth Square after Saskia, my rabbit, died,
watching the Chinese man talk crazy to me as long
as I faced him. Between him and the row of pines
(with poplars behind), a man sat on the concrete shaking
as Saskia did, marring the lotus he was making. The trees
are good, I thought, even though they don't shine.

I went at random into a store directly behind me.
A man came forward and asked, What do you want?
What do you have? I said. I sell things
for the living and the dead, he answered. And I said,
I want to buy those things. Two women at the rear
were eating soup, sucking on the crab shells. I bought
a pink dress made of paper with pomegranates on it.
Paper things of red with green and black and yellow.
I bought money for the ghosts and the spirits,
remembering the fig leaf falling that morning
just before I covered her with dirt. A day I touched
life twice. One real, one of paper. One for myself,
one for both realms which want to touch.

That was the religious part. But Saskia is dead
and might die. By fear and memory. She might die
and that softness go away. Nothing to be done.
The fog comes in. Can we let memory suffice? Is it
possible to keep the body with itself? Hands holding dirt.
The poplar trees not shining behind the dark pines.
The man on the concrete shivering. The custard pie I ate
after, which cost sixty cents in the Chinese coffee shop.

64

Custard and coffee and memory and presence. The spirit
of her soft fur and the body hardened by death.
Myself who isn't anything stopped yet. Who must learn
everything over because she is another with my memory.
Taken away. Mostly lost. The geraniums I put on her,
paper heart, paper fish, lots of mint. Five-fingered fern
and the leaf that fell from the tree by itself.
My heart is vacant. My position like a rabbit.
My eyes vacant, blurring her in the light.

ALMA IS WILLING

She is willing to grow larger. Put forth leaves
and apples. Preside over disputes of snake with man.
Symbolize with her life the ruin of time's management.
She is half the material of happiness.
Half a symbol of the best things destroyed. All of this
because her roots are underneath the earth
while her eminence is high and the sun holds her to it.
To its ride and rule. So she must choose and choose,
die and regain the muscle and purity of everything.
Harvest apples in the fall before frost comes
to turn the firm fruit to mush.
Fragility even in something so good and round.

PRAISING SPRING

The day is taken by each thing and grows complete.
I go out and come in and go out again,
confused by a beauty that knows nothing of delay,
rushing like fire. All things move faster
than time and make a stillness thereby. My mind
leans back and smiles, having nothing to say.
Even at night I go out with a light and look
at the growing. I kneel and look at one thing
at a time. A white spider on a peony bud.
I have nothing to give, and make a poor servant,
but I can praise the spring. Praise this wildness
that does not heed the hour. The doe that does not
stop at dark but continues to grow all night long.
The beauty in every degree of flourishing. Violets
lift to the rain and the brook gets louder than ever.
The old German farmer is asleep and the flowers go on
opening. There are stars. Mint grows high. Leaves
bend in the sunlight as the rain continues to fall.

TWELVE YEARS AFTER THE MARRIAGE SHE TRIES TO EXPLAIN HOW SHE LOVES HIM NOW

Beyond the mountain is a meadow with iris.
The shade of the firs determines the measure
of their color. Violet so pure the purple
is almost not there. The difference
between air and the sky's blue.
The iris hold color because they are a thing,
but mysteriously, making both the substance
and the invisible more clear.